DIFFERENT DRUMMERS

Don Caron and Lyle Hatcher

Sound Enterprises inc. Publishing
Copyright © 2009 by Don Caron and Lyle Hatcher

Publishers Cataloging-in-Publication Data

Caron, Don and Hatcher, Lyle
     Different Drummers / Don Caron and Lyle Hatcher
     1st Edition – Spokane, Washington
     SEI Publishing
     www.seizoom.com

Fiction/Biographical/Christian/Family Life

ISBN 10: 0981963609 (h.c)   0981963617 (s.c)
ISBN 13: 978-0-9819636-0-0 (h.c) 978-0-9819636-1-7 (s.c.)
EAN: 52395 (h.c)   51495 (s.c)
LIBRARY OF CONGRESS CONTROL NUMBER: 2009923323

Editing by Anne MacIver
Cover design and layout by Tami Rotchford
Authors' photograph by Mary Gladhart
Cover photograph by Allison Achauer
Printed and bound in the USA
Special thanks to:
     Jack LaLanne   Derek Kavanagh
     The Dahlke Family   The Caron Family
     The Hatcher Family Gary and Lisa Marks
     Maria Baker

NOTICES
Excerpts from *The Jack LaLanne Show*, copyright © 2005 BeFit Enterprises. Used with permission. Jack LaLanne photo © Be-Fit Enterprises. Used with permission.

Published and distributed by SEI Publishing
www.differentdrummersbook.com

CONTENTS

When the boy and the dog reach the wide expanse of the open meadow, their pace temporarily slows. Lyle stops and bends down, hands on his knees, needing air but not tired. He can see the Log from here, across the meadow, and he keeps his eyes on it, holding his focus. Dino lets loose with an excited bark and runs ahead, already sure of their destination.

Lyle isn't ready. He throws his hands out wide, palms upward, and turns his face into the sun. He stands like that, perfectly still, and then suddenly reaches out and grabs a wild sunflower, crushes it in his fist, and holds it close to his face. He breathes deeply, taking in the pungent odor of the fading summer.

Dino barks again, and Lyle scatters the remains of the flower into the wind and breaks away at a full sprint, pushing until he can no longer feel his legs moving. His eyes squint and his hands stretch open and without slowing he throws his head back and shouts, "You wanna run? Let's run!"

Out of the corner of his eye, he glimpses motion, and he turns to find David catching up to him in smooth, long strides, so easy, so relaxed. Lyle, with his short legs, knows David can easily outpace him, but he doesn't. He matches Lyle's speed perfectly, and as they move in unison, they glance at each other and their faces break into wide grins, uncontainable, both of them reveling in this incomparable sensation, this wild exhilarating freedom.

The sky is a luminous blue, the trees are every green imaginable and the boys are running so fast, the meadow floor has become a magical dazzling haze of all shades and shapes winging past them, gliding beneath their feet. They race toward the Log with a reckless fervor, as if they had waited a lifetime for this precise moment—this one chance.

CHAPTER ONE

FALLING

If a man does not keep pace with his companions,
perhaps it is because he hears a different drummer.
Let him step to the music which he hears,
however measured or far away.

~ HENRY DAVID THOREAU

1965

Nestled at the foot of the Bitterroot Mountains in Northern Idaho along the shoreline of Lake Pend Oreille, is a four-thousand acre refuge known as Farragut State Park. There's a hidden natural wonder in this park: a spacious meadow formed in the shape of an enormous amphitheater, circled by a protective forest of stately pine, aspen and Western larch. It's an ideal location for camping, isolated and sheltered, with plenty of space, and ready opportunities for every conceivable outdoor activity.

One nippy morning in early September, the thirteen members of Pack 221, the Tenderfoots, crawl from their tents and scurry about, starting their fires and preparing their breakfasts.

Mr. Evans, a former Marine turned Scoutmaster, and Mr. Gallagher, his assistant for the weekend, have been up for quite a while. They stand, slumped against the morning chill, sipping their instant coffee and watching the Scouts at work.

"Where's Hatcher?" Mr. Gallagher inquires. "Haven't seen hide nor hair of him since he came boltin' outta that tent a half-hour ago."

"No, and you won't," Mr. Evans chuckles. "I needed a break, so I sent him off for some firewood. That kid is busier 'n two tomcats in a gunny sack."

Mr. Gallagher grins. "Busier 'n a peg-legged pirate in a room fulla rat traps."

"Busier 'n a fart in a skillet," Mr. Evans fires back.

"Why, he's busier 'n a one-eyed man in a—"

"All right, all right, we got kids around here! That little varmint's gotta be kept busy, that's all."

The men enjoy a hearty laugh while Lyle, the Scout they're discussing, scrambles up the steep hill sloping toward the rim above the camp. He sports a flattop crew cut, slight fangs and bright, clear-blue eyes, and he's short for his age of ten—the shortest Scout there. A hatchet in his hand and determination on his face, he moves quickly up the hillside without stopping to rest. It's a long climb and he likes it.

Wood rats last night, and chipmunks at sunup. Squirrels droppin' pinecones on the tent. Bombs away! Rabbits sound like babies cryin' when the coyotes kill 'em. Frankie had to run and sleep in the grownups' tent. The rest of the Scouts stayed awake, but I was too tired to worry.

Crows yellin', "Strange boy, boy in the woods!" The winds cover me up and hide me. I'm safe up here.

Man, I wish Jimmy would quit snarfin' his nose. Quit it! Quit snarfin'! If Mike says, "I can't do it" one more time, dang it, I'll just go help him! I feel bad for him, anyway. He's no crybaby. His dad never goes to any of the Scout stuff. Everybody else's dad goes, why doesn't his?

Crispy burnt bacon, fried potatoes, and little tiny cereal boxes from Kellogg's. I'd like three, please. No, wait! Make it four!

Lyle arrives, breathless, at the top of the hill. There, looming above him, is the reason for his efforts: a colossal standing-dead Ponderosa pine, well over sixty feet high. He spotted it from the camp first thing this morning, and it had "a weekend's worth of firewood" written all over it.

Lyle's eyes travel to the top. He expended a lot of energy on this climb, and the effort triggers self-reflection. He realizes he's completely worn out his welcome with all of his friends. It's not his fault, really. It's simply that people have trouble keeping up with him. But whatever the reason, a guy will do almost anything for friendship, and as he stands gazing up at the giant tree, he thinks, what his friends need right now is firewood, and lots of it. It doesn't occur to him there could be difficulties chopping through the enormous trunk with a tool designed for little more than splitting dry kindling.

He winds up and swings with such force that the hatchet glances off the bark and flies out of his hand. He spins around to check if anybody noticed. A squirrel chatters noisily at him, then scampers up a nearby larch and vanishes from sight.

Lyle retrieves the hatchet, digs his feet in, and hacks away at a frantic pace, switching hands as needed to avoid slowing down. Bark chips and wood shavings scatter to the ground. The distant sounds of the Scout camp float up from the bottom of the bowl and echo back from the opposite rim.

> *Sure glad I'm not down there, fakin' havin' a good time. Tyin' knots, who cares? How to trap and skin animals? If I was hungry, I'd kill a deer. Not sure how, I just would . . . Holey smokes! There's one right now!*

Lyle sights a doe, lying in the tall grass rimming the upper edge of the basin. The camouflaged animal would be invisible to almost anyone else, but to him it stands out as if in thick, dark outline. Colorblind, Lyle knows only shapes, textures, and patterns. "Color" is an indistinguishable muddle for him, with the single exception of blue—that gloriously inviting, drinkable, swimmable, irresistible, blueberry blue—the exact color of this morning's sky.

The sun is high enough now, above the hills, to cast the golden glow of morning down into the camp. The warm air, true to Indian summers in the Northwest, settles onto the forest like a comfortable blanket. Lyle breathes it all in.

Gotta love the smell of those campfires. Smoke follows beauty and me. Mr. Evans says it keeps the mosquitoes away. They don't bite me anyway 'cause I have anti-mosquito blood.

Musty sleepin' bags, canvas tents and propane. It puffs when you light it with a wooden match. Blue flame with a yellow tip like candy corn. Stare right at the lantern and you can't see at all. Watery hot chocolate, graham crackers with Hershey's and burnt-to-a-crisp marshmallows. If you just toast 'em golden brown you're a wuss or a girl.

Repetition has refined Lyle's hacking into actual chopping, and the chopping sends wood chips rocketing in every direction, filling the air and littering the ground. The morning breeze rustles through the trees, drawn from the hills by the warm sunlight striking the cool water of Lake Pend Oreille.

Most people woulda quit by now but this is the easiest way to get a lotta firewood. Besides, the guys'll think this is the coolest!

When a tree falls, wait 'til it almost hits you, then move fast at the last second. Don't be scared 'til I'm scared! I never exaggerate, swear to God!

Lyle focuses on the motion of the hatchet and finds a rhythm, steadier and less frantic. His arms are tired but he doesn't slow down—doesn't even consider it.

CRACK!!!

The sharp noise splits the air like a gunshot and echoes against the opposite side of the meadow. Birds fill the sky in a noisy flurry and swiftly disappear over the ridge. Lyle stops. He waits. He can hear the voices from the camp below, distant and indistinct. He listens, but he can't make them out.

Swinging the hatchet out wide, he puts every ounce of effort into another hit. The tree responds with an unearthly rumble. Lyle waits again, and then lifts his hatchet. As he is about to strike, the tree interrupts, emitting a crackling sputtering groan that starts quietly and quickly crescendoes into a frightening roar.

Lyle leaps up and backs away, awestruck by the immensity and power of the sound. The massive tree slowly leans and twists and begins to fall. The wind takes hold of its boughs and it topples, tearing off the higher limbs of its neighbors, ripping larger and larger branches from the surrounding trees with the enormous force of its descent, finally slamming heavily into the ground and bouncing sideways in a roaring din of breaking branches and splintering wood.

The thunderous noise attracts the attention of the entire camp. Everyone freezes, staring up at the crest of the hill. The tree has landed parallel to the hillside and lies there, in plain view of the Scouts below. Lyle clambers up on top of it, waves the hatchet above his head, and screams out a high-volume Indian war cry. It echoes for miles.

Standing on the downed tree, he goes to work hacking off the branches. The first few come away easily, but when he encounters one of the larger limbs, he struggles. After chopping into it from the top, he attacks it from one side and then the other. Growing impatient, he kicks down at the limb, throwing all of his weight against it. The branch snaps. The tree takes a forward turn and pitches him over backwards onto the ground.

Lyle watches in horror, as the tree meets the downward slope and takes another slow roll . . . and then another, as if testing its newfound freedom. He springs to his feet and tears after it, clinging to the trunk and digging his fingers into the bark in a desperate attempt to stop it.

"No, no, no, no, no!"

The tree flips over, again, then again, gaining momentum. It leaps and bounces down the hill, throwing up chunks of turf and dirt as it rips a fast path through the steep meadow. Lyle chases after it in a panic, waving his arms above his head.

"*Run!* Run for your lives!"

The pine collides with an enormous rock outcropping and the impact launches it into the air. The top snaps off in its own direction while the main trunk smashes into the ground, rolling directly at the camp.

Mr. Evans, alerted by the threatening rumble of the tree's approach, swings around to see a fifteen-hundred-pound rolling pin bearing down on his troop. To the right, he finds all the color drained from Mr. Gallagher's face. To the left, the Tenderfoots are huddled, paralyzed in their tracks.

The sound of a whistle pierces the air. Mr. Evans shouts an order:

"Run for the trees!"

The Scouts waste no time scrambling for cover.

Lyle's feet scarcely touch the ground in his frenzied flight after the tree. He trips and falls but jumps back to his feet, falls again, accidentally somersaults, and manages to land upright, running. Unable to keep up, he's still charging down the hill when the tree reaches camp, blasting through the tents and fires, crushing and mangling everything in its path.

When it finally rolls to a stop, there is complete silence. A single cricket chirps once. It's as if every trace of life in this previously protected place has been swept away. Campfires have been smothered and are mere wisps of smoke. Smoldering ashes scatter about the area and dust drifts up and swirls away in the breeze. Tents are flattened and backpacks squashed and mauled. There's not a sign of a Cub Scout anywhere.

The long silence gives the campers the courage to emerge, cautiously, from behind the trees and out of the underbrush. Mr. Evans rises from his post behind a large rock and storms directly up to Lyle.

"Sac-ra-men-to-Ca-li-for-nia! What were you thinking? Look at this! *Look at it!* Are you out of your mind?!"

"I was gettin' some firewood. For the whole 221," Lyle offers sheepishly, pointing to where the tree came to rest at the opposite side of the camp. "See? It's dead."

"*It's* dead? We could all be dead, for cryin' out loud! Just . . . just put your things in your pack! I'm takin' you home."

Numb, Lyle gathers his camping gear together and stuffs it into his mangled backpack. Mr. Evans opens the trunk of his car and directs Lyle's movements with terse gestures. Lyle tosses his backpack into the trunk, climbs into the passenger seat, and waits there for Mr. Evans.

Seventy-five miles away, Miss Dorothy O'Donnell is alone in her office. She moves about the room with a nervous feminine grace, yet almost manly authority. Late forties, tall and fit, she wears her hair tight in a bun, knotted and pinned stiffly in place. Her clothes are neither designed nor worn with an eye to attractiveness, casting her rightly as a spinster. A radio plays from somewhere in the room. The KJRB newsman's resonant voice relaxes her.

A new package of number-two pencils rests on the desk. While she listens, Miss O'Donnell slips a pencil from the pack, inserts it into the sharpener, and slowly turns the crank. She removes it, confident it will have a perfect conical point, which it does. She cleans the pencil with a quick puff of air and places it neatly in her center desk drawer, where she lines them up like a well organized infantry, awaiting orders.

If Dorothy O'Donnell loves anything, it is this school. Linwood Elementary is her domain, and she runs it not unlike a general. Her strict authoritarian methods have earned her the nickname "DOD Almighty." The teachers whisper it, invariably with respect and admiration, but only among themselves. Despite their efforts to hide it from her, she knows. Nothing escapes her attention.

The newscast ends and the programming shifts to music. Miss O'Donnell switches off the radio, and basks in the silence. Out in the hallways, the doors are closed, as they always are when classes are in session. It is so quiet here, someone entering might think it to be a vacation day. Closed doors and absolute silence are two of her many regulations. This is her school, and those are her rules.

A door opens, and breaks the peace. An eleven-year-old boy exits his fourth-grade classroom, relying on the wall for support. His skin and face shine, practically glow, and his hair is an unusual brownish yellow color, like a perfectly drawn choirboy on a Christmas card. His body is long and gangly, and he has the unmistakable loping stride characteristic of muscular dystrophy.

The journey from classroom to restroom is a long one for David, and today he finds it even more trying. Throwing one leg in front of the other and sliding his hand along the wall, he persists until finally he arrives at the bathroom. The door feels heavier than usual but he wrests his way inside. He balances against the sink to rest.

Glancing up, he catches his reflection in the mirror. Beads of perspiration form on his forehead and trickle down his cheeks. He'd like to reach up and wipe them away, but he's afraid to let go of the sink. Instead, he lowers his head and watches the droplets plop into the bowl, winding around on the smooth surface until they disappear down the polished chrome drain.

David inhales, then makes his way along the row of sinks, using them for support. He stumbles and catches himself, avoiding a disastrous fall, but he's unable to regain his balance. His heart pounds as he struggles to stand upright, pushing forcefully against the porcelain surface.

Something in his body has changed, and he refuses to give in to it. Holding himself up with his arms, he waits for the muscles in his legs to respond, as they always have before. Arms quivering, he grows even more determined. When the quivering intensifies into spasms, David feels control slipping swiftly away, and despite excruciating effort, his arms and legs give out. He collapses to the floor and lies there exhausted, breathing labored, too tired to move. His clothes are damp from the prolonged exertion. They cling, sticky and heavy to his skin.

David isn't frightened. He knew someday this would happen. The doctors warned he would eventually lose the ability to walk without assistance, and sometime after, the ability to walk altogether. He just hadn't expected it so soon. He hadn't expected it today.

Lying with his cheek to the floor, he contemplates the perfectly straight lines of shiny tiles, and he's grateful Mr. Merrick keeps it so clean. The cold surface feels good on his skin, cooling his body and relaxing him.

Inevitably, energy returns. He rolls to his stomach, spreads his legs apart, and pushes himself up onto his hands and feet. He developed this trick as a way to stand up, but this time he falls. He makes another attempt, then another, and is forced by exhaustion to rest. It's now very clear—he is not going to stand, yet he has to get back to the classroom for help.

David struggles to the exit and heaves his body into a sitting position. He grabs the handle and opens the door, just enough to slip his hand around its edge. He pushes away as forcefully as he can, and falls over onto his side. The door swings back and closes on his body, trapping him.

He waits for his breathing to ease back to normal. Gathering his strength, David drags his legs free. Once in the hall, he rests again, then slides along the floor, working himself forward on his elbows. It's a slow and laborious process, but he focuses on the glow he sees coming from the doorway at the end of the hall. He stops several times to rest, and finally reaches the classroom.

David taps quietly on the doorframe, waits several minutes, then taps again. He taps and waits . . . taps and waits . . . until Mrs. McGuire glances up and notices him. She rushes over and drops to her knees.

"Goodness, gracious! Why didn't you call out?" she exclaims, her voice full of concern and compassion. She lays a comforting hand on his back.

"I didn't want anybody to see me," he admits shyly.

Without getting up, Mrs. McGuire swings around and speaks with hushed urgency to the student in the desk closest to her.

"Jimmy, go get Miss O'Donnell! Quickly, now!"

At the Hatcher residence, in a quiet suburb of North Spokane, Lyle's older sister, Linda, sits on the couch in the living room, doing homework. A car pulls into the driveway, and she unfolds from her comfortable spot. Tall for her age of thirteen, the tallest girl in the entire school, she has perfect posture, which exaggerates her height even more. Linda kneels on the couch by the window, edges the drapes aside, and peers out.

"Mom?" she shouts at the kitchen. "When's Lyle s'posed to get home?"

"Sunday night," Mrs. Hatcher calls back. She winks at her husband. "The calm before the storm," she adds with a grin.

Lyle's younger brother, Steve, hops up next to Linda at the window, excited at the possibility of entertainment. They watch together, as Mr. Evans opens the car door and Lyle climbs out and retrieves his backpack. Pieces fall off and the crushed canteen bounces from the driveway. Mr. Evans, obviously drained, shuts the trunk.

Eight years old, with white hair like Linda's, Steve is something of a sight to behold: skinny and bowl-legged, with corrective shoes shaped in such a way they appear to be on the wrong feet. (The neighbor lady sometimes intercepts him on the way home from school and very helpfully switches them.) He leaps off the couch and rushes to the kitchen to deliver a live report for his parents.

"Well, he's here right now, and somebody squashed his canteen!" Steve announces, as if taking credit for the event.

"That was a brand-new canteen," Mrs. Hatcher frowns. She grabs a dishtowel and hastily dries her hands.

"Yeah, I know—brand-spankin' new!" Steve buzzes back to the window to gather another update.

Linda glares. "Don't have a cow, Steve."

Steve ignores her, reporting again to the kitchen. He raises his volume a notch. "Scoutmaster Evans is mad!" He flies to the couch for another peek and then starts toward the kitchen again, almost shouting this time, "I think he's in really big—"

"Steve! That's enough." Mrs. Hatcher enters the room. "Ron, will you see what's going on, please?"

Linda stays perched at the window as her dad walks out the door and down the sidewalk, with Steve tight on his heels.

Mr. Hatcher stands in the driveway talking quietly to Mr. Evans. Steve gloms onto Lyle, who drags his backpack toward the house.

"Hey, what happened?" Steve asks, following him through the front door.

"Nothin'."

Linda's tone is gentle, concerned. "You okay, Lyle?"

"Did ya get in trouble? Huh?" Steve demands.

Suddenly, Mr. Hatcher looms in the entryway. He closes the door a bit louder than necessary. It gets everyone's attention.

"Dad, it wasn't—"

"I don't even want to hear it."

"But Dad," Lyle explains, "all I was doin' was gettin' some firewood and the wind—"

"Mr. Evans tells me you cut down a tree right on top of the Scout camp." Mr. Hatcher shoots a look at his wife.

"No, no, that's not how it happened. I didn't cut it down on top of the camp, Dad."

"You're grounded for a week."

"But Dad, I—"

"Did you hear me?! One more word outta you, and it'll be two weeks."

"Okay, Dad, I know, but I'm tryin' to tell ya—"

"Two weeks, then! Now go to your room!"

Lyle slumps down the hallway.

"And take this thing with you!" Mr. Hatcher grabs the backpack off the floor as if it weighs no more than a feather and holds it out in Lyle's direction. Lyle turns back, takes the crumpled pack from his dad, and drags it down the hall into his bedroom, closing the door.

Mr. Hatcher thrusts a forefinger in the direction of his two other children. "You two. Go to your rooms. Go on!"

Linda immediately obeys.

"But Dad, I wanna listen," Steve objects. "Anyway, I—"

"To your room!" Mrs. Hatcher halts him mid-sentence.

The parents wait for the bedroom doors to close. Mr. Hatcher, six foot two and over two hundred pounds, strong as an ox and towering in the small kitchen, leans and puts his hand on the table, waiting. His wife stands ramrod-straight, sixty-one inches of fearless authority. He admires her in so many ways, and at the moment can't help notice that the pretty Mrs. Hatcher has a perfect hourglass figure.

Her words yank him back to reality. "What next?"

Mr. Hatcher's frustration floods back. "Why doesn't he ever think about the consequences?"

"Because he's ten years old?"

"I don't care if he's ten years old. He could have seriously hurt someone. You don't see any of those other Cub Scouts cutting down trees on top of the camp, do you? They're ten years old!"

"You're always telling our kids, 'Don't be a sheep, don't be a follower.' At least he gets that part right." She stifles a grin. He's not amused.

"There's gonna have to be some changes." Mr. Hatcher grimaces. "This kinda thing can't keep going on like this."

David sits on his living room couch, observing, as Dr. Metcalfe carries a brand-new, folded wheelchair through the doorway and leans it against the wall. The doctor kneels in front of David and methodically checks the flexibility and muscle response in his legs.

"David, we need to talk about where this is going."

He flexes the boy's foot. David searches the doctor's face.

"Did my mom tell you what happened at school today?"

"Yes. She did. It's something we've been expecting. Your muscles continue to grow weaker. Tell me about your exercises. Have you been good about those?"

"We never miss a day, right, Mom?" David responds, incongruously upbeat.

Mrs. Dahlke smiles.

"You've done a great job, no doubt about it." Dr. Metcalfe agrees. "I want you to keep that up, and we'll be adding a few more. Now. I need you to promise me something." Dr. Metcalfe rises. He opens the wheelchair, and pats the seat cushion into place. "Promise me you're not going to get any speeding tickets in this thing. What do you say?"

Mrs. Dahlke hurries in to help, as Dr. Metcalfe maneuvers David into the chair, swings the footrests into position, and lifts David's feet, placing them on the rests.

"Why don't you take it for a test drive? I need to talk to your mom for a minute. Okay? Be careful now, son."

David slides his hands over the wheels, as Mrs. Dahlke and Dr. Metcalfe step onto the front porch and close the door. Mrs. Dahlke stares at the sidewalk, deep in thought. Dr. Metcalfe waits, aware that she wants to say something.

"Will he ever walk again, Doctor?" she eventually asks, meeting his eyes.

He hesitates. "No, Mrs. Dahlke, he won't. Not without help."

"When I took him to Salt Lake City," she begins, tentative, "the doctors there said they'd have a cure in eight years. It's been seven, now. Have they been able to . . . ?"

"It's tough, Mrs. Dahlke. Believe me, I know. But hang in there. The research is ongoing, and you never know."

He pats her arm, and moves down off the porch.

"Dr. Metcalfe?"

He stops, turning back.

"Thanks for stopping by. And . . . thanks for bringing the wheelchair."

"No problem. I was on my way home. If you need anything at all, give me a call. Oh—Mrs. Dahlke?"

He pauses.

"I've worked with a lot of patients over the last thirty years. That boy of yours?" Dr. Metcalfe smiles kindly. "He might surprise us."

CHAPTER TWO

THE TROUBLE WITH DANCING

I have learned to use the word "impossible"
with the greatest caution.

~ WERNHER VON BRAUN

The gymnasium at Linwood Elementary is busy, as it is every Tuesday morning at ten o'clock. This is a time every child in the school anticipates with great enthusiasm. This is the day Mrs. Maxfield teaches dancing.

Mrs. Maxfield sashays into the gym with striking grace and elegance, a flamboyant, energetic woman in her mid-forties. She wears a full-bodied midi-skirt lavishly decorated with hand-painted flowers, and her jet-black hair is neatly wrapped into a French bun. As she sets her portable record player on the stage, her smile—today as every Tuesday—betrays the absolute delight she feels . . . for Mrs. Maxfield has a secret.

When she interviewed for her post as the fifth-grade teacher at Linwood Elementary, she was prepared to be persuasive. Her husband was out of work and she was desperate to be hired. But when Miss O'Donnell informed her they were searching for someone who could also teach dancing, Mrs. Maxfield's persuasiveness astonished even herself. She didn't hesitate to proclaim that *she*, Madge Maxfield, had the background and experience for the job.

For Miss O'Donnell, finding a qualified teacher who could also cover dancing was an enormous relief. What she didn't know—what brings the smile to Mrs. Maxfield's face this and every Tuesday—was that Mrs. Maxfield had never danced a step in her life.

Hired on the spot, she wasted no time ensuring she could deliver on her claims. She rushed home and rifled through *The Spokesman–Review* in search of a coupon she had noticed when she read the morning paper.

> **Learn to dance in twelve easy lessons**
> **at the Universal Dance Studio**
> **in Downtown Spokane.**
> **Twelve classes**
> **for only twenty-five dollars.**

The following Monday, she signed up at Universal and took her introductory dance lesson, and the next morning stood in front of her new students in the Linwood gymnasium, ready for her first session as a dance instructor. She fell in love with the teaching, with the dancing, and with the children. Mrs. Maxfield was hooked.

Today, hardly any of the students notice Mrs. Maxfield's entrance because they're captivated instead by Jason's attempt to conquer the peg climb. Resembling a gigantic, horseshoe-shaped cribbage board fastened to the wall, the climb has holes running up the left side, across the width and down the right; the challenge is to use the two pegs as movable hand-holds while attempting to navigate the entire route.

Jason is dangling part way up, his legs flailing as he struggles to yank out a peg, insert it in the next hole, and make his way to the top.

"Come on, Jase!" George encourages.

"He ain't gonna make it," Billy predicts. "No way."

Billy, utterly convinced neither Jason, nor anyone else in the class, can complete the peg climb, has confidently bet a pack of Red Hots on the outcome. Jason manages to move up to the next notch, eliciting yet another rallying comment from George. He hangs there for a while, but his legs aren't moving anymore. He falls to the floor, and the kids respond with screams and groans.

"I told ya." Billy says. "Nobody ever does it. It's impossible."

Lyle steps up and jumps at the pegs but he's too short to reach them. Jason and Billy make stirrups with their hands and give him a boost, and he just manages to get the pegs inserted back into their starting positions when Mrs. Maxfield interrupts. She claps her hands together sharply to get everyone's attention. Billy and Jason drop Lyle to the floor, and the three of them hurry to join the other students.

"Good afternoon, ladies and gentlemen," Mrs. Maxfield sings in her Southern Belle lilt.

"Good afternoon, Missus Maxfield," the children sing back to her in unison.

Unison, that is, with the exception of one—that one being Lyle. His full attention is on Sharon Anne, a cutie with mousey brown hair and a pretty smile.

"Now children, please line up. We have an exciting hour of dancing before us. Can you feel the energy? I can. Good posture, now, big smiles!"

As Mrs. Maxfield speaks, she demonstrates clearly and precisely what she expects from the children. At Universal Dance Studio, the instructors, whether dance experts or not, know how to act the part. She faithfully imitates what she has seen there, giving the children the full benefit of her observations. She stands with her back erect, head up, shoulders down, and chest lifted.

"Puff up like a bird," she says, and does so herself.

In fact, she does look like a dancer and the smile comes naturally as she gazes around the room, checking to see how well the children emulate her. They love her, and even Lyle would normally be trying very hard to please her, if he weren't so distracted by Sharon Anne.

Mrs. Maxfield removes the sleeve from the record that she uses for class: *Blame it on the Bossa Nova*. Lyle pays close attention as she eases the disk over the spindle and lifts the needle.

He's figured out a plan, and he's confident he's positioned himself perfectly for it. His feet are already moving in short kicks and pops, and he's vigorously shaking his hands, like he's trying to dry them. He's ready to dance . . . with Sharon Anne.

Mrs. Maxfield places the needle onto the record and the familiar choir of scratchy static warms up the speakers.

She claps out the count, "And five . . . six . . . seven-and-eight-and . . ."

The dance begins. Instantly, Sharon Anne is swept away and disappears into the throng of weaving and bobbing heads. Lyle tries to keep track of her, but it's like watching a teacup ride at an amusement park.

> *Dang it! I can't see her. Oh, wait! Here she comes. Nope, there she goes. Now she's gone. Oh, there she is! Here she comes, closer and closer and . . . dang it! Where'd she go this time? Where did she go? Oh! Yes, yes! There she is. This time for sure. Yes! Whoops! You gotta be kiddin' me! Gone again?*
>
> *Bam! Bama-rama-ding-dong! Holey smokes, I'm dancin' with her! I'm dancin' with Sharon Anne!*

He fixes his gaze on the blue barrette in Sharon Anne's hair. It plays a familiar trick on his eyes. She seems to be standing motionless, as the rest of the room swirls around them.

> *She's got those tiny hamster ears. Freckles on her nose. C'mon hands, warm up! I swear I can't hear anything. No sound. Say somethin', you dope. My heart's gonna jump right outta my chest and hit her*

square in the eye like a frog's tongue! Gross! Good gravy, focus. What would Fred Astaire say?

She smells like ivory soap and powder, she smells like a warm wind and flowers. I don't know what kinda flowers. Just some flowers that smell really, really, good type smelling flowers.

Her breath is like steam out of an iron. It's milk in the morning, warm toast with homemade strawberry jam. Her breath is like . . . it's like . . . it's like Cocoa Puffs. Yeah, that's it, Cocoa Puffs. Man-oh-man, I love chocolate!

Lyle bumps into the dancers behind him, and it snaps him out of his daydream. He's clutching Sharon Anne in a clumsy grip, almost a bear hug, and he stumbles over her feet, causing a traffic jam.

Sharon Anne tries diplomatically to extract herself, but finally has to say something to get him to release his hold.

"Do you mind?"

The music ends and she scuttles to another part of the gym, straightening her dress and hair, searching for her friends.

Eyes on fire, Lyle races toward the cinderblock wall at full speed. He takes a giant leap and smacks into the peg climb as he grabs both of the pegs in his fists.

"Got 'em!" he exclaims, only to himself.

He swings his body recklessly, inserting a peg and lifting himself up, yanking the other peg out, hitting the next hole, and lifting, again and again. He's completely focused and fully engaged in his wildly fun private party. He reaches the top, easily navigates across to the other side, and starts back down. By now, all the kids are gathering to watch.

He finishes without a miss, pops both pegs out at the same time by pushing his feet against the wall, and drops to the floor, pegs in hand. He indulges in a ridiculous victory dance while the kids go wild, screaming and shouting and dancing along with him. There's no stopping him now. He puts the pegs under his shirt, imitating Mrs. Maxfield's posture and physical stature.

He puffs up like a bird, and with his peg-breasts and best Southern Belle accent says, "Can you feel the energy? I can. Good posture, now! Big smiles!"

The other kids respond with gleeful shrieks. Sharon Anne turns away in disgust. She isn't the only one who is unimpressed.

A voice cuts through the din.

"Mis . . . terrrr . . . Haaaatcher!"

The gymnasium is instantly silent. Lyle glances around and startles to see Miss O'Donnell hovering over him, arms folded in front of her like General George Patton. Lyle has noticed she has an uncanny way of showing up at the precise times he'd prefer she did not.

"Mr. Hatcher?" she says firmly, "I have a plan for you."

Lyle stares at her, slowly lowering his left hand, causing his pointy left breast to sink to his waist.

"Are you listening to me?"

Lyle nods.

"Good! You will be running to school in the morning. The bus is off limits to you. And I don't want to see you walking, either! You will be running! Is this clear?"

"Yes, Miss O'Donnell!"

Lyle tries to extract the other peg but it's so tightly wedged against his skin, his efforts make it appear there's a wild guinea pig loose under his shirt. Miss O'Donnell winces at the sight of it. She reaches out her hand, impatiently snapping her fingers.

"Hand over those pegs, before you put somebody's eye out," she demands in a stern voice.

Lyle works the peg free, and hands it to Miss O'Donnell, who's clearly relieved to have it over with.

"And another thing," she continues. "Tomorrow you'll spend recess in the boiler room! And right now, two laps around the playground!"

Lyle doesn't move a muscle.

"Now!"

He jumps and bolts out the door.

Down the hall in the fourth-grade classroom, Mrs. Stewart, familiar to the students as an occasional substitute-teacher, sorts through neatly organized stacks of papers on Mrs. McGuire's desk. Tonight, she'll write to her husband at his post in Vietnam, and let him know of her good fortune in landing a temporary teaching job. But right now she is preoccupied as she prepares to teach on very short notice.

Mrs. Stewart has taught Mrs. McGuire's class before, and she particularly enjoys it, though she's aware she has big shoes to fill with this job. She knows how much the children adore Mrs. McGuire—not only the fourth-graders, but all of the students in the school.

The only other person in the room with Mrs. Stewart is David Dahlke, sitting in his new wheelchair near the window. An opened book lies on his work tray, and David contemplates a full-color rendition of the solar system while he draws his own version on a sheet of blue-lined notebook paper. He stops working for a moment to listen to the noises drifting down the hall—children laughing and playing in the gym.

"Sounds like they're having fun," he comments to Mrs. Stewart.

"You may wheel down there and watch, if you want to," she offers.

"No, it's okay, Mrs. Stewart. I really want to finish this."

David returns to his drawing and then interrupts himself again. "Mrs. Stewart?"

"Mmm?"

"I'm really glad we have you for a teacher when Mrs. McGuire's not here."

"Why, thank you, David! So sweet of you to say. I'm sorry she's gone today, I know you're all awfully fond of her. She's not feeling well. Something's going around, I guess. We'll make her a card this afternoon, how would that be?"

David nods.

"Have you had the flu yet this year, David?"

He shakes his head.

"No, I don't usually get sick like that."

He turns to the window and spots Lyle on the perimeter of the playground, running, with several dogs chasing behind him. Lyle stops, picks up a pinecone, and throws it straight up in the air. The dogs bark wildly and dart in circles, ready to pounce on it the moment it lands. Lyle gazes upward, and lets the pinecone fall directly toward his face. At the very last second he moves out of the way, and zooms off again, dogs in hot pursuit.

David cranes forward to keep Lyle in sight . . . and loses him as he and the dogs round the corner of the building. He angles his wheelchair to see if Mrs. Stewart witnessed this peculiar bit of theatrics. She did not. Her attention is on the children flooding back into the room, energized from their dancing, faces flushed.

Moments later, Lyle charges in. The exertion doesn't seem to have slowed him down. Mrs. Stewart intercepts him before he gets far.

"Lyle, you have a new desk. I've got you up here, in the front row."

"Did I do something wrong, Mrs. Stewart?"

"Please collect your things and bring them with you."

Lyle gathers up everything in his desk, wanting to be sure he only has to make one trip. One is more than enough, when you're suddenly the center of this type of attention. As Mrs. Stewart leads him to the front of the classroom, he turns his head toward the windows and squints at the playground, pretending there's something intriguing out there, hoping everyone will wonder.

Tile, tile, tile. Step on a crack, break your mother's back. Black shoe scuff. Mom always says, "Pull your shoulders back and walk like a king. People will think you're important."

I'm thinkin' I hate the front row. The front row is for teacher's pets, and for kids who need glasses, and for cheaters . . . or kids with a problem. Does Mrs. Stewart think I cheat?

The teacher helps him get situated in his new location, next to David. Lyle adjusts the desk to make it perfectly square with the tiles. He arranges his things and takes inventory. Pencils are sharpened and sit small to tall.

"We'll pick up right where Mrs. McGuire left off. Page twenty-seven in your history books, please," Mrs. Stewart announces to the class.

"Dang it. I forgot mine," Lyle blurts out, actually surprised he can't find it.

Mrs. Stewart steps over to David's desk and says quietly, "David, would you mind sharing your book with Lyle today?"

David shakes his head, and Lyle scoots his desk closer.

Satisfied the issue has been resolved, Mrs. Stewart continues with her lesson plan. She writes a question on the chalkboard in large block letters, all capitals.

She presses too hard on the chalk and makes a screechy noise. Why does she do that? Mrs. McGuire never makes that noise when she writes on the board. Those letters are way too up-and-downie. Her fingernails are all chewed. I wonder if she knows what she's doin'.

Lyle starts to feel anxious. Mrs. Stewart moves away from the chalkboard, her question completed:

WHO INVENTED THE VACCINE FOR POLIO?

She turns back to the class and says, "Please read, beginning on page twenty-seven, and quietly raise your hand when you know the answer."

Lyle's apprehension grows. The question on the chalkboard looms, rolling itself into the room, taking over the space, demanding to be answered. Lyle's eyes are intently fixed on David's book, but he can't concentrate. The letters will not form into words. His eyes feel lazy.

Stale air in here, rose perfume and oatmeal stinkers. Tap-tap of pencils, snarfin' sounds, and the pages shooshin' when they turn. I can smell tunafish sandwiches.

Hands pop up all around the room as the faster readers find the answer. Mrs. Stewart waits for everyone before she continues.

Michael breathes too loud. He always sounds that way. Why does he leave his crayons on his desk like that? They're gonna roll off. Nerdling, put 'em away! You're not colorin' anything! I had special crayon holders in the second grade with the colors written on 'em in big letters 'cause I'm colorblind. That was the year Suzy wet her pants. Nobody ever forgets that.

David leans over to Lyle and whispers helpfully, "Are you done yet?"

David's words, even with his gentle delivery, strike Lyle's ears like an accusation from a judge in a big black robe. He thinks of *Perry Mason*, not one of his favorite shows.

"No, I'm not done!"

"Do you need some help?" David asks.

Irritated, Lyle shakes his head and makes another effort to read. He can make out the first word, "the", and then his mind drifts back to the Suzy incident.

> *It sounded like spilled milk at the dinner table, runnin' to the center where the big crack is, drippin' down and puddlin' on the floor. It was an awful lot once she started and she kept goin' and goin'. Good gravy, Suzy . . . you're makin' us feel weird . . . can you just clench?!*

"Are you having a problem with it?" David inquires politely.

"I don't have a problem. What's your problem?"

"What do you mean, what's my problem? Are you talking about—?"

"I mean, what's your problem?!"

"Shhh. You're going to get us in trouble. We're supposed to be reading."

"Readin'? Hey, I can read. I have a focusing problem. Not a stupid problem. Focusing."

Mrs. Stewart glances over at them and shakes her head.

"That's not what I meant," David tries to explain, "and now you got us in trouble."

"Did not."

"You did."

"Did not."

"Yes, you did."

"Not!"

David squirms in his wheelchair.

"Shhh. Okay. You didn't. Please be quiet."

"You be quiet."

"Excuse me, Mrs. Stewart?" David says quietly.

"Yes, David?"

> *Oh, great! That's just great! Here we go again!*

"Are you squealin'?" Lyle whispers at him, worried.

David ignores him.

"May I go to the restroom, please, Mrs. Stewart?"

"Of course. Lyle, would you go with him?"

Lyle sits, staring after David as he wheels himself away from his desk.

Wow, he's not a squealer!

"Lyle, did you hear me? Go with him, please!"

David is already at the door. Lyle springs to his feet and catches up with him.

Outside the classroom with the door closed behind them, Lyle scans for opportunities—so much freedom, so many possibilities—until he realizes there's nothing here but an empty hallway with no one in it, and his attention shifts back to the only thing of interest: David's wheelchair.

"Hey, how fast d'ya think this'll go? Like maybe twenty miles an hour?"

"It's not for racing," David replies, patient and matter-of-fact.

"I know. I know that! But what's the fastest you've ever gone? I mean if you're really goin' fast, like super-fast, how would you stop it?"

"It has brakes, right here." David points out the handles, situated above each wheel. "But it's not for racing."

Lyle jogs backwards up ahead, facing David, already filled with his own ideas, an enormous grin on his face.

CHAPTER THREE

THE FEELING

True friendship is a plant of slow growth.

~ GEORGE WASHINGTON

*T*a-tap. *Ta-tap.* The distinct echo of high heels drifts from down the hall and around the corner, breaking into Lyle's reverie.

"Oh no!" he exclaims.

"What?" David worries, mainly because of the look on Lyle's face.

Lyle yanks open the bathroom door, and whispers urgently, "Get in there. Fast!"

Again they hear the shoes, closer this time. *Ta-tap, ta-tap.*

They hustle into the room, and Lyle drops to the floor. He scopes out the perimeter from under the door, watching as a pair of high heels passes by. Abruptly, he jumps up, startling David.

"Duke!" he shouts into the corner of the room.

"Duke . . ." The tiled wall responds.

Obviously, he's done this before.

"Puke!" he shouts.

"Puke," echoes the wall.

He throws his voice into the corner, with staccato force, singing his improvised lyrics to the popular tune, *Duke of Earl.*

"Puke-puke-puke, puke of hurl, puke-puke, puke of—"

David glances around the room, shifting nervously, as though he expects Miss O'Donnell to beam herself into the urinal stall.

"Don't worry. She's not gonna come in here. Miss O'Donnell. Ughh!"

"I like her. I think she's nice."

"Why don't you just marry her then?"

David rolls his eyes.

"That's what I thought," Lyle grimaces.

David chooses to ignore the comment.

"Hey, I was just wonderin', how come you were walkin' at the beginning of school and now you're in a wheelchair?"

"I have muscular dystrophy."

"So you can't walk anymore?"

"I can still walk, but I have to have help with it."

"What's gonna happen?"

"Nothing. I just have to do my exercises every day. Hey," David says, intentionally changing the subject, "I saw you running out there on the playground during dance class."

"Oh, that. It's not what everybody thinks. I'm not in trouble or anything."

"You're not?"

"Heck, no. See, I got this thing. It's kind of a problem. My brother calls it *the feeling.*"

"Okay, well, I was wondering about it. I mean what's it like?"

Lyle thinks for a moment.

"You know those little drummers? The kind you wind up?"

"Yeah," David says. "I have two exactly like that at home. They're dogs."

Lyle stops short. "Are you sure they're not bears? I mean, I've seen wind-up bears but I've never seen wind-up dogs. You sure they're not bears? 'Cause if—"

"They're dogs," David insists.

"Okay, fine then. You know when you wind 'em up, and you wind 'em, and you wind 'em, and you wind 'em?"

Lyle demonstrates the winding with quick flicks of his wrist.

"And then, when you let 'em go, they go like this?"

He moves his arms in a slow jerky robotic style, getting faster and faster until he works himself into an insane seizure of frantic, flailing air-drumming. When he stops, David stares at him in disbelief.

"That's what it's like? Are you kidding me?"

Lyle widens his eyes and stares directly into David's pupils.

"Nope, I'm not kidding. That's exactly what it's like."

David shakes his head. "How could it be like that? It doesn't look anything like that when you're doing it."

"Doin' what?"

"Running," David replies, astonished that Lyle has already forgotten what they're talking about.

"Running?" Lyle asks with surprise. "I thought you were talkin' about *the feeling*. You don't know what running's like? Haven't you ever run before?"

"Not really. I mean not like you do. I always walked kind of funny, you know, because of the muscular dystrophy. You run more than anybody I've ever seen."

"Oh, anybody can do that."

"Even me?"

"Oh yeah, you could do it! Definitely!"

David suddenly remembers why he needed to come to the restroom in the first place, and squirms.

"Would you please hand me the tube? In the green thing?"

Lyle checks the back of the wheelchair and locates a green fly-rod sleeve. Curious, he slides it out, opens one end and peers inside. He removes a long neoprene tube, and brandishes it overhead, like a swordsman testing a new blade. As he swings the hose, the motion creates a distinctive sound and pitch, feeding a sense of power and excitement in him. He swings it faster and faster, trying to force the sound even higher.

Shwoop. Shwoop! Shwoop!

"Don't move," he commands David. "I promise I won't hit you."

David, immediately nervous, sits with his back erect, completely immobile.

"Stop!" he says stiffly, moving only his lips. "I need that!"

Lyle misinterprets the calmness of his response as encouragement. He whirls the hose even harder.

Shleeep, shleeep, shleeep, shleeep!

Now it's moving so fast it's almost invisible and it sounds like a dangerous power tool on the loose.

"Stop it! Please!" David begs.

Lyle stops, but instead of handing it over, he puts it to his lips and sings into it, half megaphone, half trumpet.

"Puke-puke-puke, puke of hurl—"

"Stop it. Please give it to me!" David insists.

"Sorry. I was just havin' fun. What's it for, anyway?"

Lyle holds the tube out to David, an apology on his face.

"It's my urinal tube. Give me a sec, okay?"

David takes the tube from him and proceeds to use it for its intended purpose. As comprehension dawns, Lyle puckers. He spits and wipes his mouth on his sleeve, making a face as if he bit into a raw lemon.

David diplomatically changes the subject.

"Hey, I was talking to Mrs. Stewart, the substitute teacher, this morning while you guys were dancing in the gym."

"Yeah?"

"Yeah, she's nice."

"I like Mrs. McGuire better. She's actually my favorite teacher . . . ever," Lyle replies wistfully.

"Me, too," David agrees.

Lyle opens the door to the hallway and holds it while David wheels himself through.

"She's pretty, too," Lyle reflects.

David and Lyle are certainly not alone in their feelings regarding Mrs. McGuire. She *is* a very pretty woman, and has a bright smile she wears often, but those are merely hints of a deeper attractiveness, an almost magical quality, that makes children want to be close to her. If she is on the playground during recess, a crowd of kids always swarms her.

"I wonder when she'll be back," Lyle ponders.

"She's sick."

"Yeah, I know. What's she got?"

Lyle lets the door swing closed. The boys move slowly down the hallway in the direction of the classroom, in no particular hurry to get there.

"I don't know what she has," David tells him. "But . . . I know she's not going to make it."

"Not gonna make it to what?" Lyle asks, confused.

"Oh," David says, turning his face to Lyle, with a sudden expression of sadness. "What I meant was . . . umm, she's going to die."

A peculiar sensation stabs Lyle, a dull prickly vibration. It travels through his entire body, from his scalp to the bottoms of his feet, leaving an unpleasant and sickly feeling in his chest area. A frown clouds his face.

"What . . . are you . . . *talkin'* about?!" Lyle challenges David angrily. "That's the craziest thing I ever heard. Nobody can tell that. You don't know! Anyway, who told you that? The doctor?" Lyle pauses for a quick breath. "Did the doctor tell you that? What's his name? I wanna call him, right now!"

"It wasn't a doctor." David says, surprised at Lyle's outburst.

"Okay, then," Lyle says.

David isn't certain he should share how it is he knows about Mrs. McGuire. He thinks about it and hesitates, but decides it's the right thing to do.

"God told me," he says simply.

Lyle is stunned. He's never had to take on God before.

"Wait a minute. God told you?"

David nods, slowly.

"Mr. McGuire called me last night, and told me she was in the hospital. And he asked me to pray for her."

"Why would he call *you*?"

"I don't know."

The answer pacifies Lyle, easing his anxiety about David's dire proclamation.

"People call me, too," he tells David. "To find lost stuff in the woods, 'cause I can see everything. I found two watches, a wallet with seventy-eight dollars—seventy-eight, can you believe it? And I found earrings, and keys, and money, and I even found a diamond ring once. Oh no, wait a minute. I didn't find the wallet with seventy-eight dollars in it. Actually, my brother, Steve, found that . . . umm . . ."

Lyle pauses, deep in concentration. David waits patiently. Lyle blurts out, "But I *was* the one that pushed him into the bushes where he found it, so . . ."

David bursts out laughing. Lyle laughs too, choosing to believe the laughter is David's admission he's mistaken about Mrs. McGuire.

In the classroom, Lyle plops into his seat next to David. The two of them go back to reading from the history book, but neither is thinking about history. David considers telling Lyle the rest of it—about how people call him to pray for them because they believe he has a "special relationship with God."

Doris Greer was the first to call, a few years back, when she learned she was dying of cancer. She requested David pray for her, sharing that she desperately wanted to live long enough to raise her two boys. David went into his room and turned out the lights. Later that night, he assured his mother that Mrs. Greer was going to be fine.

He wonders what Lyle would say if he told him about that. David clearly remembers the surprise on his mother's face, even if she did try to hide it, when at the age of four he explained to her that God talked to him. He glances over at Lyle, who is wiggling in his chair.

Mrs. Stewart notices. "Lyle? Please try to sit still," she warns, though her tone is gentle.

Lyle tries, but he can't stop thinking about what David said. He wants to, but he can't.

> *What did he say about Mrs. McGuire? What were*
> *his exact words? "I don't know what she has. But I*
> *know she's not going to make it."*

Lyle shakes his head, trying to force the thought to leave him alone.

> *That was just crazy! People can't say stuff like*
> *that. He doesn't know. Nobody can know that! Not*
> *even doctors.*

Lyle sneaks a look at David, who is now deeply engrossed in the history book. Lyle squirms again, and the words he doesn't want to hear—or even think—come to mind despite his efforts to hold them down.

> *"God told me." Ergghhhh! Well even if God did tell*
> *him, there's still gotta be a way to stop it!*

"Dang it!" Lyle blurts out, thumping his fist on his desk.

"Lyle!" Mrs. Stewart scolds in a forced whisper. "I warned you once."

"I'm sorry, Mrs. Stewart."

"Do you need something?"

"No, thank you. I'm sorry, Mrs. Stewart."

Lyle forces himself to hold very still in his chair, but he can't keep his mind from racing.

After school, Lyle beelines for home. There are questions to be answered. Big questions!

At the crosswalk, a happy-looking yellow lab, panting with his tongue hanging out, sits across the street next to the fire hydrant, waiting patiently.

Lyle lets out a high-pitched whistle, giving the dog permission to bound across the street and jump on him. He showers Dino with a good scratching, not even slowing down to do it.

"Hey, boy. C'mon!"

When they reach the Hatcher house, they charge across the yard, leap onto the porch and burst through the door into the kitchen. Lyle's mom juggles the last-minute dinner preparations. She doesn't miss a beat.

"Hey! Slow down and put the dog back outside. I don't like him begging. And then go wash your hands and help your brother set the table." She sips from a spoon to taste-test the sauce she's preparing.

"Mom, do you believe in God?" Lyle dives in.

Mrs. Hatcher chokes on the sauce, spilling some on the stove's burner where it sizzles as she spins to face him.

"Lyle, what have you done?!"

"Nothin', Mom. That's not what I meant. I just need to know 'cause this kid at school says God talks to him! I'm not makin' this up. He really said that!"

Relieved, she regains her composure and snaps back to her tasks.

"Well, honey, then I think you should ask your friend at school more about it. How would I know if God talks to him or not? I can tell you one thing I do know. It's time for dinner, and I'm saying it for the last time. Wash your hands and help your brother set the table!"

"But Mom—"

Mr. Hatcher's voice booms out from the next room.

"Lyle! You heard your mother!"

Lyle shoots from the kitchen, question unanswered.

CHAPTER FOUR

THE WEASEL

Don't think to hunt two hares
with just one dog.

~ Benjamin Franklin

L yle wakes up feeling out of sorts. It's not clear to him what he's troubled about, though he knows he didn't sleep well. He plods quietly into the kitchen, thinking no one else will be up, but Mrs. Hatcher is at the kitchen table, studying.

"Hi, Mom."

She reaches out and gives him a hug, still engrossed in her studies. Lyle drops into a chair and watches her, knowing better than to interrupt. Early morning is her private study time, and she has often made it clear that without it she will never earn her teacher's certification.

Footsteps sound in the hall, and Mrs. Hatcher tilts up her gaze with a smile. Typically, by this time of the morning, Mr. Hatcher has been at work for several hours, milk truck loaded, delivering his route, but not this week. Every six weeks he has five days off, the result of his six-day work week. More often than not, he works these days for the extra money, but today he shuffles into the room to enjoy the luxuries of sitting at the breakfast table and reading the paper.

In no time, the kitchen buzzes with morning activities, as Mrs. Hatcher deftly manages the challenge of getting the children off to school.

"Mom?" Linda asks. "Can you give me a ride to the leadership conference after school tomorrow? I've been nominated for treasurer."

"I'll pick you up at three." Mrs. Hatcher says, drawing Linda close. "Good job, I'm so proud of you."

This bit of extra attention to Linda does not go unnoticed by Steve. "I need a ride to Jo Albi Stadium on Saturday. I'm gonna win the punt pass and kick again this year!" he proclaims with confidence.

Mr. Hatcher delivers Steve a stern gaze. "Son, we've talked about this before. You shouldn't get so cocky. Practice and hard work. That's the ticket, and you know it."

"Okay, Dad."

Lyle digs in his pocket and comes up with a brand-new, yellow merit badge. He holds it out proudly.

"Got my survival badge. What d'ya think of that?"

Linda pats Lyle's flattop haircut, as if he's a good luck totem of some sort.

"G'bye Mom, 'bye, Dad," she says, as she gathers her things and slips out the door.

"I thought you got kicked outta the Cub Scouts," Steve challenges Lyle, trying to start something.

Mrs. Hatcher quickly interjects. "Let's not even get into that. Steve, go to your room and get your shoes on. You're going to be late."

Steve moves to do as he's told, but Lyle stops him.

"For your information," he tells Steve, "I didn't get kicked out. I'm just takin' a break. I'm kinda busy with other stuff right now."

"Yeah? Like what?" Steve grills. "Sharon Anne?" Steve packs his voice with as much ridicule as his eight-year-old imagination can muster. He plugs his nose when he says her name, for extra effect.

Lyle can't let it go. He grabs Steve around the neck and administers a noogie.

"Ow, Lyle!" Steve whines, loudly. "Ow, ow, ow, ouch!"

"That's enough!" their dad snaps. "And by the way, Lyle, if we get one more report from Miss O'Donnell about trouble at school, you can forget about any fishing trips to Pend Oreille!"

"Dad! I don't mean to do it."

"Yeah," says Steve, his voice spooky. "It's *the feeling.*"

Steve apes an exaggerated version of a frustrated Lyle, wrenching his face up like a bulldog, stiffening his neck and face muscles, and wildly flexing his fingers.

"Nice, Mr. Funny Pants," Mrs. Hatcher observes dryly.

Steve embellishes his imitation even further. She suppresses her laugh.

"Now that's enough of that! I know what it's like. I have the same thing only I get it in my feet." She points a slender finger at Lyle. "But it doesn't mean I go around stomping on people."

"That's funny, Mom," Lyle grins.

Steve darts to his bedroom and back, shoes on his feet, says his goodbyes and wanders out the door. The television in the living room is on, and Mrs. Hatcher warms up for her daily exercises with *The Jack LaLanne Show,* stretching while listening to the fast-paced, high-energy coaching.

Everyone knows better than to mess with Mom's "out of the house by eight o'clock" routine. Lyle is the exception to her rule. He stays, mesmerized by Mr. LaLanne's voice, and watches right along with her, up to the very last minute. At 8:15 sharp, he'll dart out the door, arriving at school seconds before the final bell rings.

Jack LaLanne captivates and motivates people merely with the sound of his voice, as millions of women across the country—

at this moment foregoing coffee and donuts for morning exercise—can attest. But this isn't why Lyle loves his show.

Lyle's fascination stems from the stories he's heard about Mr. LaLanne, such as his swim across the Golden Gate channel while towing a 2,500-pound cabin cruiser, and another from Alcatraz Island to Fisherman's Wharf he accomplished while handcuffed. In Lyle's eyes, these are feats that would challenge even the characters in his favorite comic books.

More importantly, Lyle feels a strange kinship with Mr. LaLanne, possibly because he promotes many of the same lifestyle choices Lyle is familiar with through his mom's rules: no sugar, lots of exercise, regular sleep, and healthy food.

If this was just some boring old guy crusading against junk food, Lyle would be down the street faster than you could say "Twinkie." But in Lyle's mind, Jack LaLanne is a true-life hero: a living, breathing example of How Anything Is Possible. As Lyle listens, he thinks of what happened yesterday in school.

"If you want a miracle, you have to have the intestinal fortitude and willpower to do the right thing. But you have to do it. I promise if you will just dedicate a few minutes a day, you will get results. A few minutes. That's all I ask.

"And please, please remember, if you're going to improve yourself there's only one time that's important. You know when that is? It's not Christmas. It's not New Year's. It's NOW! N-O-W! Are you with me? All right.

"And I want you to remember this, too. When you set a goal for yourself, get that picture in your mind and focus on it every single day when you get up and every night when you go to sleep. You let your mind and your body know that's the picture you want for